T0057415

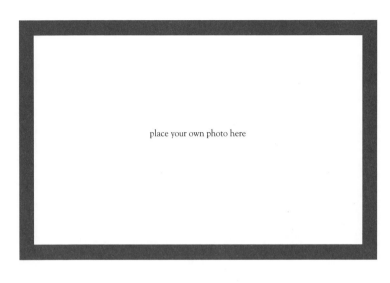

place your own photo here

A special gift for

_____

with love,

_____

date

_____

For Ryan, Asa, Aslyn, and Aevin. You are the greatest scrapbook material! I love you!

Stories, sayings, and Scriptures to Encourage and Inspire

hugs™
for
Scrapbookers

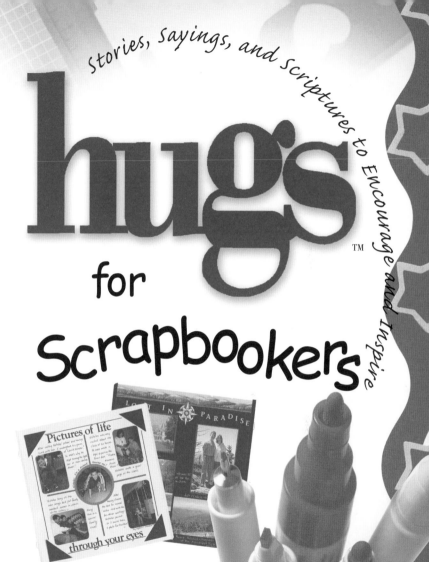

STEPHANIE HOWARD

Personalized Scriptures by
LEANN WEISS

 HOWARD PUBLISHING CO.    CREATIVE memories™

Our purpose at Howard Publishing is to:
• *Increase faith* in the hearts of growing Christians
• *Inspire holiness* in the lives of believers
• *Instill hope* in the hearts of struggling people everywhere
Because He's coming again!

Hugs for Scrapbookers © 2005 Stephanie Howard
All rights reserved. Printed in China
Published by Howard Publishing Co., Inc.
3117 North 7th Street, West Monroe, LA 71291-2227
www.howardpublishing.com

05 06 07 08 09 10 11 12 13 14   10 9 8 7 6 5 4 3 2 1

Paraphrased scriptures © 2005 LeAnn Weiss
3006 Brandywine Dr.
Orlando, FL 32806; 407-898-4410

Edited by Between the Lines
Interior design by Stephanie Walker

Library of Congress Cataloging-in-Publication Data
Howard, Stephanie Lynne, 1974–
    Hugs for scrapbookers : stories, sayings, and scriptures to encourage and
inspire / Stephanie Howard ; personalized scriptures by LeAnn Weiss.
        p. cm.
    ISBN 1-58229-448-8
    1. Memory—Religious aspects—Christianity. 2. Scrapbooks. I. Weiss,
LeAnn. II. Title.

BV4597.565.L96 2005
242'.68—dc22

                                                                    2005040368

This book was created in association with Creative Memories. Creative
Memories® is a registered trademark and business unit of The Antioch Company.
To learn more about Creative Memories, visit www.creativememories.com. A
special thanks to Creative Memories for several of the photos in this book.

*We do not remember days,
we remember moments.*
Cesare Pavese

Contents

Chapter 1: Staying Connected 1

Chapter 2: Bringing Healing 17

Chapter 3: Providing Support...............................35

Chapter 4: Investing Yourself 53

Chapter 5: Reviving Old Feelings 71

Chapter 6: Protecting What's Important...............89

Chapter 7: Giving Love 107

Chapter 1

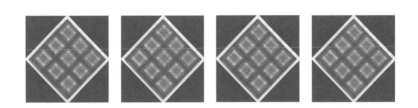

Staying Connected

You're unforgettable to Me. I've engraved you on the very palms of My hands. I'll never leave you or abandon you. You can always count on My unconditional love and goodness.

Eternal hugs,
Your Heavenly Father

—from Isaiah 49:16; Deuteronomy 31:6; Psalm 23:6

Have you ever noticed the immediate connection you have with someone once you learn that she scrapbooks too? With that discovery two strangers instantly connect. Suddenly they have plenty to talk about. "How many books do you have?" "How often do you work on them?" "What kind of journaling do you do?"

There are so many things to ask and learn from a fellow scrapbooker, and it's quite likely that the conversation will end with an invitation to work on albums together in the future. Many new friendships have formed in the process of sharing ideas and trying new techniques. It's not unusual to find that as you craft your pages and memories together, you're crafting relationships and sharing joys.

Scrapbooking with others is a great way to stay connected too. Often we get so busy taking care of our families and their busy schedules that it's hard to find time for friends. Sometimes the only opportunity we have to catch up with them is when we get together to work on our albums. Friends can work side by side, arranging their favorite photos while catching up on the happenings in each other's lives.

Scrapbook albums help us stay connected here and now, and they help us stay connected to our past as family and friends relive their adventures and strengthen their ties with us any time we flip through the pages. And scrapbooking also helps us connect with others to enrich our future.

Aren't you glad you're connected?

*There can be no happiness equal
to the joy of finding a heart
that understands.*

Victor Robinson

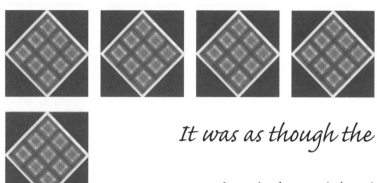

It was as though the

final thread had

been severed. Tessa

wasn't sure she

could keep this up.

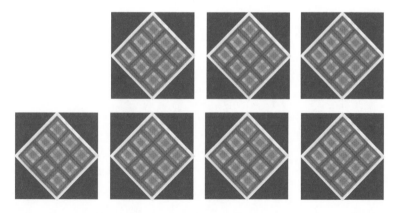

Thursdays with Ina

"Hey, Tessa! I've been looking for you." Tessa had just locked her dorm room when she saw her friend Pam coming down the hall.

"Hi, Pam. What's up?"

"A bunch of girls are going to a movie tonight. You want to come?"

Tessa crinkled her nose apologetically. "Sorry, not tonight. I was just leaving to scrapbook with Ina." Tessa had a standing appointment with her grandmother most Thursday evenings.

"Oh, that's right. I forgot it's Thursday. How's she doing these days?"

Tessa smiled even as she felt a twinge of discouragement. "As well as can be expected. Some days are better than others."

Ina had Alzheimer's disease. For a while Tessa's family had taken Ina into their home. But when Ina started wandering in the middle of the night and taking extra doses of medicine, the family had made the difficult decision to place her in a nursing home.

Now, every available Thursday evening, Tessa packed up her scrapbook supplies and went to visit Ina. Unfortunately, Ina's illness had slowly stolen her ability to enjoy most of her favorite leisure activities, but she still showed interest in scrapbooking—even if she sometimes mixed things up or forgot what she was working on. Reviving their shared hobby was Tessa's effort to help Ina remember things through family photos.

Ina had stopped recognizing her granddaughter a few months ago. Although Tessa had known to expect this, it still felt disconcerting. That was one of the reasons she called her grandmother by her first name. Sometimes Ina's confusion caused her to become agitated when she didn't recognize family members. It just seemed easier to avoid that if possible.

Tessa felt strongly about continuing their hobby together, about trying to preserve some sense of connection, but as Ina's memory deteriorated, their meetings seemed to have little purpose. It was as though the final thread had been severed, and terrible as she knew the thought was, Tessa wasn't sure she could keep this up.

She arrived at Ina's room just after the dinner hour. It was a small space, yet cozy. Besides the green recliner, a bed and dresser were the only other pieces of furniture. The window valance and bedspread were of the green toile fabric Ina had chosen and sewn herself years ago to complement her favorite chair. Tessa and her family had tried to bring as much familiarity to Ina's new surroundings as possible.

Knocking on the open door, she greeted Ina with carefully constructed cheerfulness. "Hi, Ina!" The tiny but spry woman was seated in her green recliner, watching a bird perched outside the window.

Ina turned to see her visitor. "Well, hello, dear. Have you brought my supper?"

"No, Ina, supper is over," Tessa explained patiently. She motioned to her scrapbook tote. "I've come to show you my scrapbook. I thought maybe you could help me with my pictures today."

With a look of pure delight, Ina stood up and welcomed Tessa into her room. "I would love to!"

Tessa smiled. One thing Ina hadn't lost was her enthusiasm.

Then Ina placed her hand on Tessa's shoulder. "I seem to have forgotten your name, dear."

Tessa swallowed, frustrated that she'd been caught off-guard again. Their re-introduction had become part of the routine. She should have been expecting this. "I'm Tessa, your granddaughter."

Ina seemed confused but not bothered by her failed memory. "OK, Tessa."

Tessa laid the scrapbook on the bed. While Ina flipped through the pages, Tessa set up the rest of her scrapbook materials.

"This is lovely!" Ina exclaimed, admiring pages she herself had helped create. "Now, who is this?" She pointed to a photo of a man and woman holding hands.

"That's your daughter Gloria and her husband, Jim—my parents."

For a moment Ina gazed at the couple as if trying

to find some missing link that would explain these strangers. Apparently unsuccessful, she simply tapped the photo and spoke matter-of-factly. "Well, they make a handsome couple. The young woman is quite pretty, don't you think? I like the mischief in her smile." She chuckled, revealing that same impish grin.

Tessa smiled and laughed. "Yes, she is." Taking her grandmother's thin, wrinkled hand, she caressed it tenderly. So much of Ina's life seemed lost, yet she somehow maintained a spark of vitality.

Ina looked at her. "What are you working on today, Ruth?" Ruth was Ina's sister, who had died when she was fifteen. Tessa tried to ignore the mistake. She opened an envelope and brought out a stack of photos from her camping trip with friends.

"We had a great time on this trip," Tessa explained as she pointed to a photo of her friend Pam sleeping alone in a large tent. "We played a joke on Pam because she wouldn't stop snoring. Before she woke up that morning, we all snuck out of the tent and arranged our sleeping bags twenty feet away from the camp, then pretended to be asleep. When she woke up and found us, we told her we'd slept outside

13

all night because of her loud snoring! It was pretty funny."

Ina laughed heartily. "Oh, Tessa, you've always been such a comic! You get that from my side of the family, you know. We were always playing tricks and jokes on each other."

Tessa was too stunned to respond right away. She glanced up at her grandmother's face just in time to see the brief moment of clarity before it faded.

Tessa turned her face slightly and averted her gaze to hide the tears that had sprung to her eyes. *She remembered.* Somewhere in that fog was her grandmother, the one who remembered and loved her.

Side by side the women worked and laughed. Tessa gave Ina some stickers of bonfires and camp paraphernalia to place throughout the two-page spread.

As Tessa finished journaling the high points of her trip, one of the nurse's aides came in to check on Ina and noticed their project. "Wow! That looks great!"

"Oh!" Ina said, looking at the scrapbook pages she'd just been working on as if for the first time. "Isn't it lovely!"

Tessa observed the look of happiness in her grandmother's eyes and had to force down the lump in her throat that made her smile quiver. Reaching for her bag, she turned to the nurse's aide. "Will you please take our picture?"

"Absolutely," the aide replied, gladly accepting the camera.

Cheek to cheek, the two women posed and smiled broadly, once for a closeup and once with their masterpiece. Ina likely wouldn't remember this day, but Tessa would never forget.

"Thanks," Tessa said to the aide. "I can't wait to show her these next Thursday."

Chapter 2

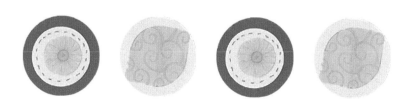

Bringing Healing

Give Me the things that burden you, and I'll sustain you. Over time I'll transform your tears to joy, if you'll let Me. You'll discover that the memory of the righteous truly is a blessing.

Comforting you,
The God Who Heals

—from Psalms 55:22; 126:5; Proverbs 10:7

Creating a scrapbook is valuable in so many ways. For one person it can be a relaxing activity. For another it might energize and inspire the imagination. Making a scrapbook can help build your own self-esteem or be used to encourage someone else. Any time energy is focused into a productive project, you're doing something good for yourself—and probably for others too.

Reminiscing is good for the soul. Just taking time out to remember what you did last summer or who came to last year's Christmas party can be a positive, enriching experience. It's fun to look back to see what has changed and what hasn't.

One of the most remarkable things about scrapbooks is that they can help people heal.

inspirational message

Whether you're creating a scrapbook or just reminiscing, the pages often hold a therapeutic, healing power.

A scrapbook can help someone who is grieving. While the pain of losing a loved one never goes away, remembering special moments with that person can help lessen feelings of loss. Although nothing can replace the unique presence of those we love, photos enable us to remember, celebrate, and communicate to others the impression they made on our lives. We can "bring back" lost loved ones just by remembering and reliving the good times we shared with them.

Reflecting on the past can be bitter-sweet, but it's the kind of pain that brings healing, peace, and restoration.

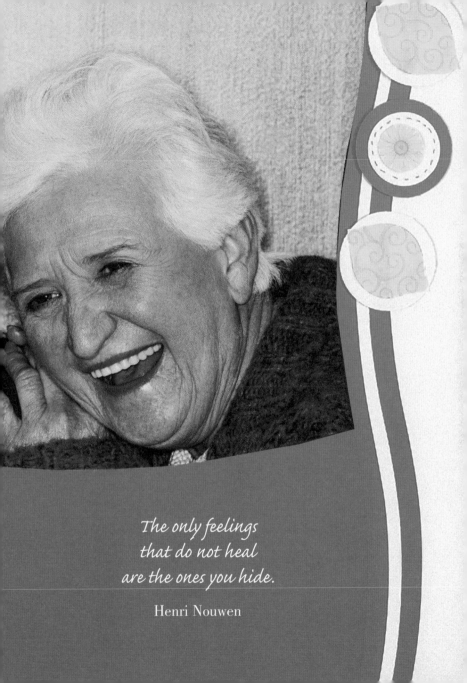

The only feelings
that do not heal
are the ones you hide.

Henri Nouwen

Sherry gasped as

she turned the

pages and saw

pictures she'd

never seen before.

Moving On

Sherry stood in front of the row of identical doors and heaved a sigh. Orange paint peeled off the storage building in random patterns. "What a run-down and dreary place," she muttered to no one.

Not that it made much difference. She planned to be surrounded by enough piles to block out her surroundings. Key in hand, Sherry opened the padlock and yanked on the door handle, waiting as the gray, metal panels rolled up out of the way.

Early morning sunlight spread quickly into the small room, casting shadows on the back wall. Sherry surveyed the large number of boxes piled almost to the ceiling and for a moment had second

thoughts about conquering the task at hand. *Good thing Mom only had a two-bedroom duplex.* Her mother had always told her she tried to tackle too much at one time, but today she was determined to get through this unpleasant task.

Almost a year had passed since her mother died suddenly from a brain aneurysm, leaving Sherry stunned and emotionally immobilized. Her mother had always been her best friend, and her absence left a huge hole in Sherry's life. At the time she was barely able to handle the funeral arrangements, much less sorting and dispersing her mother's belongings. Her only sibling, Ben, lived overseas and had only been able to come home briefly for the funeral. Her husband, Joe, had suggested storing her mom's belongings until she was ready to go through every-thing.

Sherry told herself that she was as ready as she'd ever be. She'd willed herself to keep moving through the shock and denial immediately after her mother's death, though she still couldn't shake the anger. Some days she was so angry she didn't even want to shake it. She felt cheated—her mom had been only sixty-four years old. Her rational mind knew there was nothing she could have done to predict or prevent what had happened, but she was still mad at herself for not being more attentive to her mother's health. She was angry with her mother for leaving, even though she knew that made no sense. She was angry at her brother for not being more available right after their mother's death, when she needed him most. Today she was furious to be stuck—again—dealing with the aftermath alone. And she was angry with herself for being angry with those she loved. Sometimes it felt like the guilt was the only thing that checked her growing bitterness.

But as she stood facing the daunting task of sorting through her mother's belongings, a new wave of resentment washed away even the guilt and brought back fresh anger. *Fine!* she thought. *I'll just get this over with.*

Pushing up her sleeves, Sherry started shuffling and slamming boxes marked "books" and "tax records" and "clothes" without even opening them. Adrenaline spurred her on for about a half-hour. She slowed down a little and was more careful with the boxes marked "china" and "decorations," looking

inside long enough to pull out anything she wanted to keep as a memento but not long enough to let her emotions get the best of her again.

The next box was "gardening." Her mother had loved to garden and always had a plethora of seeds and how-to guides and tools. Maybe she would keep those. But she couldn't look at them. She added the box to the modest "keep" pile.

An unlabeled box caught Sherry's attention. *Great. Probably a bunch of miscellaneous junk.* She made a few hasty slices through the packing tape. Old crochet supplies. Her mother had tried the craft but never really took to it. Sherry started to put it in the pile to donate, but when she lifted it, it seemed heavier than it should for a bunch of yarn and some guide pamphlets. *That's odd.* She set the box down again and reached inside to rummage around.

Something solid was at the bottom, and she pulled out a large black book she didn't recognize. Her pace slowed as she noted the worn leather cover. Carefully, she opened the book and discovered what must have been her mother's childhood scrapbook. Sherry gasped as she turned the pages and saw pictures she'd never seen before. She unfolded an old newspaper clipping announcing her mother the winner of a county-fair beauty pageant. Another page displayed an eighth-grade report card with "Outstanding" written in the area reserved for comments. She couldn't read the others—tears were blurring her vision.

"Ugh . . . I thought I was through with this," Sherry muttered as she briskly wiped her eyes with her sleeve. But it was no use. Fresh tears were coming before she could even turn the page. For the first time in months, she felt a chink in her armor of self-protective anger. She cleared a space on the floor and sat down with the scrapbook.

For the next hour, Sherry went through the pages, lingering over every image of her mother. She traced a finger along the edges of a photograph taken long ago and laughed aloud. It was a picture of her mother in her early teens, wearing a large, silly hat and puckering her lips dramatically for the camera. It perfectly captured the fun-loving spirit her mother had always had.

Sherry closed the scrapbook and hugged it closely. It was a part of her mother she had never

known, and it made her feel closer than ever. Suddenly she didn't feel bitter about doing this job. She wondered what other treasures she might find.

"Kitchen" was written on the next several boxes. Sherry had already collected some special things from her mother's kitchen and hadn't planned to go through these remaining trifles. Yet she couldn't resist opening every box . . . just in case. Slowly and carefully Sherry cut the tape and peered inside. She picked up potholders stained from years of baking and fingered flatware scuffed dull with use.

"No," Sherry told herself firmly as she felt her resolve waver. "I can't keep everything. Where would I put it all?" She re-taped the box and set it aside.

The next box was labeled "dish towels and table linens." *Good, this one should be easy.* But wrapped in one of the towels was the old recipe box her mother had relied on. *How did I miss this earlier?* Reverently she lifted the lid and flipped through the cards, recognizing casseroles and desserts that had been in their family for generations. Sherry smiled when she thought of all the special times she had shared with her mother, preparing meals. Her fingers lingered on the recipe box as she placed it on the growing pile of things she planned to keep.

As she pored through more containers, she lost track of time. Not until she heard the familiar chime of her cell phone did she notice that the sun was descending on the horizon. Laying down an armful of dresses, Sherry reached for her phone. "Hey, Joe," she said, recognizing their home number on the caller ID.

"Hi, sweetie. How's it going over there?"

Sherry blew stray hairs off her forehead as she surveyed the room and sighed. She hadn't even gone through half of the boxes. "Uh . . . slower than I thought, but OK."

"Are you sure you don't want me to help you?"

"No, no. I'm fine. This way I can go at my own pace." She didn't want an audience as she agonized over things like whether to keep her mother's ragged housecoat, or as she carefully preserved things that seemed silly, like the wrinkled grocery list in her mother's scribbly handwriting.

"Well, call me when you want me to pick up the stuff for the estate sale."

"Sounds good. I'll work a little longer before I call it a day."

Bringing Healing

Sherry closed her cell phone and turned back toward the pile of clothes she'd set aside. But as she scanned the piles she had yet to sort, fatigue settled in from all the tension and emotion. Strangely, though, she also felt lighter. The knot of anger that had clogged her heart for so long had dissolved.

She ran her hand affectionately over the nearest box. "For another day, Mom," she said softly. "We've accomplished enough for today."

Chapter 3

Providing Support

I've been with you from the beginning, forming you in your mother's womb. No matter where you go or what circumstances you face, you can trust Me to guide you. My right hand will support you. I'll provide for all of your needs according to My unlimited riches in glory.

Supporting you,
Your Ever-Present God

—from Psalm 139:9–13; Philippians 4:19

Anyone who loves to scrapbook knows how much more fun it is to do it with friends. In fact, anything done with others is more fun. Whether it's cooking, cleaning, or doing yard work, working along-side others makes the task more enjoyable, and the time seems to fly.

Scrapbooking is an enjoyable hobby; more impor-tantly it's an invaluable tradition that preserves the unique stories of how you live, who you love, and what you value. It does take some time though. Organizing photos, creating page layouts, and journaling all require effort and time. Many people don't scrapbook because it takes so much time.

That's why it's so good to get

together with friends to work on your albums. When you join with others, you're more likely to make it a point to set aside time to work on your photos. Friends encourage each other, inspire each other, and keep each other moving forward when it's easier to do something else instead.

Besides, it's so much fun to look at each other's pictures and hear the stories behind them. You know how much you owe your friends for sharing their great new ideas and materials to help make your pages unique and beautiful. Not to mention that you can get lots of great advice on parenting, marriage, and life in general in the process. Now, that's a support group!

*Every true friend
is a glimpse of God.*

Lucy Larcom

How could she dare admit

even to herself—much less

anyone else—that she

resented the very people and

things she loved so much?

Crop Night

Betsy sighed wearily as she put her Cavalier in park and turned off the ignition. She leaned back against the headrest and closed her eyes for one sweet moment of peace, solitude, and rest. She willed her body to move—Kimberly and Donna were waiting for her, and she was already late—but her body wouldn't obey. She was so tired, and she had already missed nearly an hour. Maybe no one would notice if she just curled up on the seat and napped.

She lifted her head and opened her eyes wide, battling their inclination to close. She knew if she didn't move now, she really would fall asleep. For the first time, she recognized that her weariness was

43

tinged with resentment—resentment of her friends for expecting her to come to something as trivial as a scrapbook night when she had so many more important things to do; resentment of her husband for encouraging—no, insisting—that it would be good for her to come tonight; resentment of all the impossible expectations life had placed on her shoulders; even resentment at little Addison for needing so much and taking so much of her mother's time and energy. But how could she dare admit even to herself—much less anyone else—that she resented the very people and things she loved so much?

She sighed again and gathered up her mountains of scrapbooks and supplies. She might as well get it over with. At least it would be one more thing she could cross off her list—if she could even find her list. She tried to at least look happy as she carefully made her way to the door.

Betsy didn't want to put down the stack of scrapbooks in her arms, so she pressed the doorbell with her elbow. As she did, a heavy canvas bag slipped from her shoulder. She shifted her weight to the other side, unwittingly causing the stuffed bag on her other shoulder to slip down to rest in the crook of her arm, almost causing her to drop the scrapbooks.

Not a moment too soon, her friend Kimberly came to the door.

"Help!" Betsy pleaded, offering the pile of books to her hostess.

With a quick hand, Kimberly grabbed the load and held an arm out to steady Betsy. "Oh, there you are. We were getting concerned. Now why didn't you just make two trips?"

Hoisting each bag onto its respective shoulder, she smiled guiltily. "I didn't think I had enough energy for another trip," Betsy confessed. "Besides, I'm Super Mom. I can handle a load bigger than that while bathing the baby and cooking dinner." She laughed as she moved inside the house. "Sorry I'm late."

Kimberly followed, kicking the door closed behind her. "No problem. Donna is already set up in the kitchen," Kimberly said, nodding toward their destination.

"Hi, Betsy." Donna greeted her friend and took one of the bags from her shoulder.

Betsy slumped into the chair reserved for her. "Hey," she sighed as if it were the first time she'd sat down all day.

"Having one of those days, huh?" Donna sounded empathetic.

Raising her eyebrows, Betsy forced a smile. "Most definitely one of those days. I left a pile of dishes in the sink, and the sofa was piled high with laundry to be folded. Addison has an ear infection, so she wanted me to hold her all day long. I couldn't get anything done!"

"Oh, Betsy!" Kimberly chided. "It sounds like you desperately need a break!"

Propping her elbows on the table, Betsy rested her chin in her hands. "That's what Chad said too. I wasn't going to come, but he practically threw me out the door. He said I was way too stressed and I needed a time-out. I didn't even know mommies could be sent to time-out!"

Donna squeezed Betsy's shoulders. "Well, I think all mommies should get more time-outs. I don't know how many times I've had to beg Tom to take the kids just so I can bathe in peace. Most daddies I know don't do sick babies. You're fortunate to have a husband who actually encourages you to go."

Kimberly nodded in agreement, and Betsy realized they were right. She halfheartedly retrieved her paper cutter. "Well, I might as well try to get something accomplished tonight. It's already almost nine o'clock. The way my day has gone, I'll be lucky if I finish anything."

"I haven't gotten much done in the past hour," Donna commiserated. "I'm so far behind!"

Pulling out a binder of stickers, Betsy agreed. "I'm glad I'm not the only one behind! Addison is already five months old, and I have ten rolls of pictures I've got to do something with. I feel so overwhelmed, I hardly feel like trying to catch up."

Kimberly encouraged her friends. "Just do a little. Even if you get one page done, you'll feel good about it. Every bit helps." She held up a two-page spread featuring photos from her family vacation at Disney World. "How does this look?"

Donna looked up from her pile of pictures. "Too cute! You guys really had a fun time, didn't you?"

The three friends fell comfortably into their

routine of cropping. For a moment they worked quietly, each focused on her own project. Betsy yawned loudly, breaking the silence. "I'm so tired! I really should be in bed. Addison still isn't sleeping through the night, and it's wearing me out!"

"Here, have a little caffeine," Kimberly said, handing her a soda and a chocolate-chip cookie. "It works for me, but then again, I get a pretty good night's sleep. Zachary still comes into our bed in the middle of the night, but at least he's tricky enough to sneak in and not make a sound. I don't wake up until his foot slaps me in the face!"

Donna groaned, recalling her own experience. "Laney didn't sleep through the night till she was eighteen months old! It was miserable. Sometimes I still wake up at 2 a.m. and think I hear my baby's cry—and she's eight!"

The friends laughed with humor and empathy.

Kimberly stifled her laugh, placing a finger to her lips. "Shh, or we'll wake up my kids! I certainly don't want to fight getting them back to bed."

They resumed their work, suppressing infectious giggles. Once again the room was filled with the familiar sounds of scissor clipping and paper punching. It wasn't long before each of them had something to show from the night's work.

Kimberly stood up to refill her drink. "That looks great!" she said, looking over Donna's shoulder.

"Let me see!" Betsy requested, holding up her own completed page of Addison's first bath.

Donna held up her page, and they exchanged compliments.

With keen eyes Betsy examined her friend's technique. Donna had mounted her sister's wedding photo on vellum. "I love that idea. I need to try it on Addison's baby scrapbook.

"Have I shown you the pictures from Addison's dedication at church? The vellum will be perfect for what I'm thinking of doing with that page."

Kimberly picked up a picture of Addison in her christening gown and passed it to Donna. "She's such a pretty baby," Donna mused.

The next photo was of Betsy's family standing before the entire congregation, praying. "That was one of the first times I'd seen you," Kimberly remembered. "I thought Addison was one of the most beautiful babies I'd ever seen, and I just had to tell you after the service."

Betsy smiled. "We'd joined the church only a few months before. It was so thoughtful of you to introduce yourself and pay such a sweet compliment to Addison. If you hadn't, we might never have become such good friends."

"Oh, you only liked me because I said you had a cute baby," Kimberly replied mischievously.

"Hey, anyone who says my baby is beautiful is my new best friend," Betsy joked. The three burst into giggles once more, this time remembering the sleeping children. "Seriously though. I was new to the church and didn't know very many people. You invited me to your house and got me working on my first album."

"I could tell you'd be a good scrapbooker," Kimberly responded with a wink.

Just then the grandfather clock chimed midnight, time to quit.

"Is it twelve o'clock already?" Betsy looked at her watch. She could hardly believe it was so late. She felt awake and rejuvenated—like she could keep right on working.

Donna closed her books and zipped up her scrapbook tote. "You look a lot better," she told Betsy. "Now aren't you glad you came?"

"Yes!" Betsy replied exuberantly. "Not only did I complete eight pages, I *do* feel much better."

As she loaded up her supplies, she realized that along with the weariness, the resentment was also gone. Working with the photos and her friends had reminded her that what sometimes felt like burdens were actually blessings. She had a wonderful, caring husband. Her baby was beautiful, precious, and whole. And she had been blessed with friends who understood what she was going through and offered the encouragement of perspective. Those things were worth remembering. She resolved to cherish this revelation in the scrapbook of her heart.

Chapter 4

Investing Yourself

Life is about more than just you. Make a positive investment by looking out for the interests of others. Live your life so that your good deeds give credit to Me, and know that I'll faithfully complete the good work I've started in you.

Investing in you,
Your Gracious God

—from Philippians 2:4; 1 Peter 2:12; Philippians 1:6

Doesn't it feel good when you've completed a scrapbook page? After you've placed that final sticker or completed the caption beside the last photo, it's so nice to inspect and appreciate your work. Seeing that special event displayed, embellished just the way you like, and being able to show it to others, brings a sense of accomplishment. Even if you didn't spend a lot of time making the page or adding a lot of extra detail, it's satisfying just to see the photos in a book instead of stuffed in a box under a bed somewhere.

Plenty of scrapbookers don't claim to be creative. But with all the die cuts, stickers, and papers available, anybody can make a great-looking scrapbook page just by putting all the pieces together and adding their own personal stories. No matter what your level of skill or effort in creating scrapbook pages, you can call it a job well done because it's your special touch—you've invested a part of yourself.

It's rewarding to look at your work and say, I did that! And isn't it fun to sit back and listen to the *oohs* and *ahhs* of approval from friends and family as they compliment you on your latest masterpieces?

Don't be afraid to invest yourself and your time in a scrapbook, and by doing so, in others. Not only are you creating one-of-a-kind artwork for your family to enjoy, you're preserving memories for yourself and for generations to come.

*The noblest question
in the world is,
what good may I do in it?*

Benjamin Franklin

Part of Jordan wanted

to be understanding

and concerned for Stacy's

feelings. Most of her

could barely see past her

own aching heart.

Torn

Jordan hugged her algebra book tightly to her chest like a shield against further attack. She was in such a hurry to leave school that she didn't even take time to put it in her backpack. She didn't want to meet anyone's eyes and have to force a smile or risk someone noticing she was upset, so she hung her head low and fought her shoulders' natural inclination to slump dejectedly. Her eyes never left the dirty, tiled floor. It was a wonder she made it through the hallways unharmed. Mechanically she made her way to the parking lot.

Once outside, Jordan scanned the cars lined up in the pick-up area. Desperately she searched for

her mother's silver minivan and then hastily fled toward it.

"Hi, Jordan!" her mother greeted her cheerfully when she opened the door.

"Hi, Mom," Jordan said quietly, dumping her backpack on the floor and sliding quickly into the seat. She closed the door and buckled her seatbelt, sinking as low as she could into the safety and protective cover of the seat.

Out of the corner of her eye, she could tell that her mom was looking at her. Could she tell? Curious, she turned to meet her mother's eyes. That one glance was all it took. Her mother's look of concern broke the defensive wall she'd carefully built up. Jordan could hold back no longer. Tears spilled from her eyes.

"Oh, sweetheart, what's the matter?" her mom prodded gently.

"This girl . . ." Jordan sniffed and had trouble continuing. "She was really mean to me today."

"Tell me what happened."

"Her name is Stacy. I don't know why she doesn't like me. I've never done anything to her!" Jordan wiped the tears away with the back of her hand in an attempt to control their flow. In broken sentences between sobs, she recounted the dreadful event. "She knocked into me on purpose. I dropped all my stuff . . . her friends were laughing . . ."

"I'm so sorry, baby." Jordan felt her mom's hand on her leg, first patting soothingly, then adding a reassuring squeeze.

"That's not all," Jordan persisted, unzipping her backpack. "Stacy picked up my folder and tore it. She said it was an accident, but she and her friends walked away laughing."

She pulled out the ruined folder. Jordan had created a miniature scrapbook page on the front. She'd meticulously placed flower and heart stick-ers around the perimeter as a border, and in the center she'd mounted a picture of her dog, Coco. Seeing the torn photo brought fresh tears.

Jordan didn't think of herself as thin-skinned. In fact, she had always been good at fending off jokes thrown her way. While she handled teasing with grace, this was one prank that had cut straight to the heart. She wasn't good at sports or cheer-leading like many of her peers, but she'd discovered a creative ability through her scrapbooks. She'd

even joined the yearbook committee to pursue her talent further. It had been exciting to finally find something she could do really well.

The car came to a halt, and Jordan was surprised to realize they were already home. Her mom turned off the ignition, and for a moment they sat in silence. When her mom did speak, her voice was calm and deliberate. "We don't know why Stacy did what she did today. We don't know what life is like at her house. It may be that she hurts others because she's hurting too. We just don't know."

Jordan met her mother's eyes and felt sustained as she continued. "I do know that God tells us to pray for our enemies. Why don't we say a prayer for Stacy? Let's also pray that you'll know what to do if something like this ever happens again."

Part of Jordan wanted to be understanding and concerned for Stacy's feelings. Most of her could barely see past her own aching heart. Dutifully Jordan bowed her head and prayed for Stacy.

That evening Jordan pulled out her torn folder at her scrapbooking table and surveyed the damage. The folder and border were a complete loss, and the photo of Coco was torn, but maybe she could rescue it by turning the torn edges into a special effect. Although still wounded at such a public and unprovoked attack, she felt a surge of joy and confidence in her ability to creatively turn even the tragedy of a torn photo into something with purpose and beauty. She waited for the inspiration to hit as it always did.

Suddenly she felt the rough outline of an idea starting to form at the edges of her consciousness. The boldness of the idea startled her, and she tried to turn her thoughts in other directions, but she couldn't. The idea clicked. It was the right thing to do.

Her hands started moving quickly, proficiently, to capture her idea on paper before it flew away. She applied stickers and die cuts and her favorite paper designs. With satisfaction and determination, she knew this would be her best work yet.

The next day at school, just after the five-minute warning bell, Jordan spotted Stacy and her crowd. Jordan's heart raced, and she pulled her books to her chest defensively. For a moment she considered ducking into the nearest classroom, but it was too late to turn back. Stacy had spotted her. She pointed at Jordan and said something Jordan couldn't hear

that evoked smirks and laughter among the other girls.

With resolve and a boldness that surprised her, Jordan stepped up to face Stacy. She thought perhaps Stacy would tear the new scrapbook page in which she'd invested so much effort and hope, but she pushed the fear aside. The momentary surprise she saw on Stacy's face gave her added courage.

"Hi, Stacy." Jordan managed to smile. "I was scrapbooking again last night. I want you to see what I made." She thrust her latest work of art into Stacy's hand, then turned and walked resolutely toward her first class. This time she held her head high and felt a spring of confidence and pride. She'd sent the bully a pointed message. However Stacy chose to respond, Jordan felt good that she hadn't let Stacy intimidate her or dictate how she'd act.

But as the day wore on, that confidence was slowly replaced with uncertainty. It was like waiting for the other shoe to drop, wondering if she might suddenly encounter Stacy around each next corner. She almost wished she hadn't done it. What was she thinking?

When the dismissal bell rang that afternoon, Jordan decided she'd better clear out fast, before she had to risk facing Stacy's group alone in the empty halls. She had just opened her locker when someone from behind her slammed it shut again, making her jump. She instantly knew it was Stacy. Being this close to her bully took Jordan's breath away. Last night this had seemed like a good idea, but now she wasn't so sure. She hoped she'd be strong enough to handle a bad reaction from Stacy. She turned with dread to face her, silently praying for Stacy and for strength for herself.

Stacy thrust Jordan's card in her face accusingly. "What's this?" She demanded.

"It's a card," Jordan responded, caught off guard by the simplicity of the question.

Stacy paused before continuing, as if confused. "Did you really make this for me?"

Jordan nodded.

"But why?"

Jordan smiled and pointed to the words written meticulously with fancy flourishes. "Did you read it? It says I want us to be friends."

"I know what it says," Stacy said impatiently. "But how can you mean that? After how I've treated you . . . after yesterday . . ."

"I do mean it, Stacy," Jordan assured her. "I don't know what I might have done to annoy or offend you, but I'm sorry. I'd rather be your friend than your enemy. Can we be friends?"

She watched as Stacy fingered the card almost reverently. "It's really pretty—and a lot of work." Suddenly Stacy seemed softer, even a little vulnerable. With growing compassion and understanding, Jordan decided her mom had been right, that sometimes bullies just need to be loved. She was glad she had prayed for Stacy and proud that she'd done the right thing.

"But after what happened yesterday," Stacy mumbled, carefully avoiding meeting Jordan's eyes. "I was so mean to you."

"I forgive you, Stacy," Jordan assured her.

Finally Stacy looked up nervously. "I would like for us to be friends."

Jordan smiled broadly. "That's great! Maybe I could show you my scrapbook stuff sometime?"

"I'd like that," Stacy said, relaxing and smiling

for the first time. "Do you want to talk about it during lunch tomorrow? Maybe I could sit with you."

Grinning widely, Jordan nodded. "That would be great!" Suddenly she was aware that the halls had emptied of students. She glanced at her watch. "Yikes, it's getting late. My mom is waiting for me. She'll probably be thinking I got mugged in here or something." She smiled again at Stacy. "I'll see you tomorrow . . . friend."

Stacy smiled. It was a nice smile, Jordan decided.

Jordan waved goodbye and raced toward the door, hugging her algebra book tightly across her chest and feeling her heart pounding wildly against it. She could hardly contain her excitement. Not only was she using her creative talents to find her own identity, she was using them to encourage others. She could hardly wait to tell her mom.

Chapter 5

Reviving Old Feelings

Remember your history and your heritage.
Reflect on the good things in your life.
Think about truth and goodness.
Contemplate things that are right, pure,
and lovely. Have an attitude of gratitude
for all I've done for you. My faithfulness is
your rock through all generations.

Blessing you,
Your God of Wonder

—from Deuteronomy 32:7; Philippians 4:8; Psalm 100:5

It feels good to remember happy moments from the past—your first date, your child's first steps, your father's proud face when you hit the home run.

Scrapbooks are a wonderful way to keep us from losing those happy memories. One simple picture can bring back a memory long forgotten. Journaling that moment helps us remember the details and emotions.

A scrapbook revives those forgotten moments of your past. Big things, small things—it doesn't matter. They're all right there in your scrapbook. The memory is safe and secure. And so is the feeling.

You'll smile remembering the romantic getaway you took with your husband on your second anniversary. You'll laugh seeing photos of

74

the silly costumes you made that took first place in last year's fall festival. You'll cry sweet tears looking back at the tiny infant you held so delicately—the baby who now towers over you.

Even remembering some not-so-good moments can be beneficial. Time has a tendency to soften our perspective on negative memories. Hopefully a bad experience will seem less terrible looking back. Or maybe you'll realize how much you've grown despite that problem, or even how what seemed bad at the time worked out for the best.

Either way, memories are a blessing. Renewing them has the potential to renew a marriage, strengthen a friendship, or recharge your life.

When work, commitment,
and pleasure all become one
and you reach that deep well
where passion lives,
nothing is impossible.

Nancy Coey

It was only 7:30 a.m.,

and she was already

running on a short fuse.

Always

"Take a bite." Vanessa held out a spoonful of oatmeal, coaxing her ten-month-old, Haydn, to eat.

Her four-year-old son, Nathan, loaded his mouth with waffles. "Mommy, look at me!"

Watching syrup drip down his chin, Vanessa tried not to be perturbed. "OK, Nathan. Now chew it up before you choke."

It was only 7:30 a.m., and she was already running on a short fuse. Vanessa and her husband, Ricky, had stayed up late arguing—again. Lately it seemed they couldn't have a normal conversation without bringing up their finances. Vanessa was making an effort not to take it out on the kids.

"Daddy!" Nathan crowed as Ricky rushed in to grab a cup of coffee.

"Hey, buddy." Ricky said, rustling Nathan's hair with his free hand. "I'm late for work. I'll see you later." He knelt down and planted a kiss on each of his sons' foreheads. Without looking Vanessa in the eyes, he brushed a kiss past her cheek, hardly making contact.

Vanessa didn't even attempt to return the gesture. Scooping another serving into Haydn's mouth, she called out, "Have a good day." But Ricky had already walked out the back door.

She felt a little guilty still holding onto a grudge from last night. They just never had learned how to fight nicely. An argument that had begun about bills had digressed to complaints about in-laws and finally to a list of each other's personal bad habits. She had to admit it had gotten ugly. But he'd been as hurtful as she'd been, she reasoned.

Vanessa didn't have a hard time staying mad at Ricky. He had it easy. He went to work eight hours a day, five days a week. Meanwhile, Vanessa stayed at home with the kids seven days a week. She cooked, cleaned, and disciplined at all hours of the day and night. It was hard work, and she felt unappreciated.

Last night's argument had started when Ricky saw how much money she'd spent that week. Not only had Vanessa bought groceries, she'd purchased a few too many items Ricky considered "nonessentials," including more album making supplies.

His criticism always caused Vanessa to become extremely defensive. Her scrapbook time was used productively to make something the whole family would enjoy and treasure for generations to come.

"Mommy, I'm done." Nathan was standing up in his chair. At the last moment, he decided it would be much more fun to jump than to climb down. He hadn't noticed the cup of milk perched dangerously close to the table's edge.

"Nathan!" Vanessa warned, a bit too late. The cup bounced onto the floor, splattering milk everywhere.

Still in his crouched landing position, Nathan looked timidly over his shoulder. "Oops."

Vanessa pointed to the living room. "Go play," she commanded. Nathan went, dejected.

Reviving Old Feelings

Getting down on all fours, Vanessa wiped up the mess, as she always did. Clearly she needed a vacation. She and Ricky would celebrate their tenth anniversary next week, but they just didn't have the money to take a trip this year. Actually, they hadn't taken a trip for just the two of them since before Nathan was born.

Vanessa thought back to the early years before they had children. They both worked full time, so they always had plenty of money to celebrate their anniversaries. They'd loved traveling to foreign countries, sight-seeing, and learning about other cultures. When Vanessa decided to be a stay-at-home mom, losing her income meant they'd have to forgo the exotic, romantic getaways.

"It's probably best that we don't go on a trip this year," she grumbled to herself. "We'd probably end up fighting the whole time anyway."

As she tossed a handful of soggy paper towels into the trash, Nathan bounded energetically back into the kitchen. "Mommy, can I paint?"

Vanessa sighed wearily. She hadn't even cleaned up breakfast, and he already wanted to make another mess. "No, honey, not right now."

"Will you push me in the swing outside?" he asked hopefully.

Watching Haydn spread a handful of mush through his hair, Vanessa felt defeated. "Can you please let me clean up the kitchen first?"

But Nathan was relentless. "Can we play cards?"

"Nathan, go into the other room," she said firmly. "Now." It took everything in her power to keep from shouting the words.

Having cleaned up the kitchen and little Haydn, Vanessa put him down for his morning nap. "Nathan, I'm ready to play now," she called. She knew it was hard for her older son to adjust to limited mommy time after being the center of attention for the first three years of his life.

She found him sitting on the floor, looking at family scrapbooks—something he was only allowed to do with adult supervision. He had wrinkled pages and damaged photos one too many times.

Instead of rebuking him yet again, though, Vanessa sat on the sofa. "Do you want to look at the pictures together?"

With a solemn nod, Nathan held out the scrapbook and snuggled close to Vanessa. She noticed that the scrapbook he'd chosen was one of the older ones. "Honey, this book doesn't have any pictures of you in it. These pictures were taken before you were born. Do you want to pick a different one?"

Nathan shook his head. "No, I want this one."

Having no energy to persuade him otherwise, she opened the book. Nathan pointed to the page he'd been looking at. "Mommy, whose dog is that?"

Vanessa smiled at the mutt she and Ricky had adopted from a shelter long ago. It had been their test to see if they were ready to settle down, stay close to home, and assume responsibility for another living being. After six months they'd returned the dog to the shelter and decided they were definitely not ready.

The next page featured a costume party she and Ricky had hosted. "Who's that man, Mommy?" Nathan pointed to a shot of Ricky dressed in a Zorro costume.

"That's your daddy." Vanessa chuckled at his surprised expression, then pointed to her younger self dressed as a senorita. "And that's Mommy."

"Wow, you look pretty—like a princess!"

Vanessa laughed softly and kissed the top of Nathan's head. "Thanks, sweetie."

She realized he'd never seen his parents dressed up in such flashy costumes. *We used to be so spontaneous,* she remembered ruefully. *So fun and full of love. It really is a shame we're not like that anymore.*

Even after Nathan tired of the pictures and turned his attention to watching through the window as a utility worker vented water from the hydrant on the corner, Vanessa continued flipping through the books. She hadn't looked at some of these albums in years. She had almost forgotten so many things. She was grateful she'd put the scrapbooks together so she could once again remember things they had done as a family, emotions and feelings that had long lain dormant.

She saw Ricky as he had been then. Perhaps more importantly, she saw him as she had seen him then— through eyes of true love and affection. It almost startled her when she looked at the most recent photos of their family—and noticed that Ricky really hadn't changed. Oh, he had a little less hair, and his middle wasn't quite as trim as it had once been. But now that she had seen Ricky through the old Vanessa's eyes, she could no longer see him in any other way.

Money hadn't been the source of their happiness in the past, she realized, and it shouldn't be now. Suddenly she could hardly wait to see Ricky again. She had to see which picture of him—and their life together—was real.

Grabbing the phone, she punched in Ricky's office number. She held her breath, waiting for him to pick up.

"Hi, Ricky," Vanessa said timidly.

"Hey, babe." Ricky sounded as if he'd been waiting for her call.

"I just wanted to tell you I'm sorry for the hurtful things I said last night. I love you, and I'm happy with our life . . . even if we don't have a lot of money," Vanessa admitted sincerely.

Before he answered, Vanessa heard Ricky release the breath he'd been holding. "I'm sorry too. You know that's all I really want—for our little family to be happy." He added, "And that we have food and a roof over our head."

"I am happy," Vanessa reassured him, choosing to ignore what she would usually interpret as a jibe about her spending. "Even if I don't always act like it."

For a moment an awkward, hopeful silence hung between them. "Ricky, I thought maybe my mom could keep the kids this weekend. We could spend a quiet weekend at home, maybe watch old movies and play card games like we used to?"

"That sounds like fun!"

"And Ricky . . ."

"Yes?"

"I want us to go through the old scrapbooks together. I think it'd be good for us to remember some important things together—like how much we love each other and what's really significant."

"I never forgot," he reassured her.

"I guess I never did either. Ricky?"

"Yes, babe?"

"Let's always remember, OK?"

"Always."

Chapter 6

Protecting What's Important

Don't settle for survival—

I've designed you for abundant

life! Because I'm your refuge, your strength, and

your ever-present help in times of trouble, you

don't have to fear anything. Seek Me and My

ways first, and I'll take care of all the rest. Keep

a balanced perspective on the things that make

an eternal difference.

Looking out for you,
Your Protecting Father

—from John 10:10; Psalm 46:1–2; Matthew 6:33; Colossians 3:2

Your scrapbooks are one of the most valuable items you own. Sure, you could get more money if you sold an antique armoire or an expensive automobile, but your scrapbooks hold so much more intrinsic value.

Besides your family and friends themselves, scrapbooks featuring your loved ones are the next closest in worth. Between those pages lie the images of your loved ones, the unique expressions and features they had at one specific moment in time. People constantly change, but photos capture and document life.

How else would the next generation believe your story about the terrible haircut your big sister gave you in high school? Or how you really did glow after delivering that ten-pound baby? Those are moments worth reliving time and time again.

The owner of a new sports car waxes and shines his investment. Special care is taken when handling fine jewelry. This is the regard we should have for our family photos, because unlike those other things, they are irreplaceable. Your family and the memories you've created together are special and worth protecting. Organizing your photos and preserving them does just that.

For you and your family, those scrapbooks—and the joy, laughter, and pain they memorialize—are priceless.

Treat them with care.

*It is the mark of great people
to treat trifles as trifles
and important matters as important.*

Doris Lessing

Bob caught Debbie's eye, and his expression was grim. "It doesn't look good so far."

The Shelter

"Oh, excuse me," Debbie said, having stumbled over a man reclining on the floor. The man pulled his legs toward his chest to let her pass. She took wide strides to avoid invading anyone else's personal space. There were people everywhere—sitting, standing, and lying down. Step by awkward step, she led her family to the other side of the high-school gymnasium, trying to find adequate space to set up camp.

She nodded to her husband, Bob, signaling that she'd found a spot. He and their teenagers, Alayna and Aiden, unloaded their bags at the designated area and together assessed their situation. They stood amid groups of people huddling, lounging, and sleeping, and felt a little uncomfortable. This would be their home for the next few days as they—along with several hundred other families—took refuge from the fast-approaching hurricane.

Just yesterday a tropical storm that was heading along the Florida coastline took an unexpected turn. Becoming fiercer than previously forecast, it was now a hurricane with winds reaching up to 110 miles per hour. Everyone along their stretch of the Florida coast had been advised to seek shelter immediately. They'd been given only two hours to board up all their windows and gather their belongings before the civil authorities had warned it would no longer be safe to remain.

The West Hills High School gymnasium was one of the makeshift shelters provided. Scanning their temporary residence, Aiden spotted a friend from school. "Hey, Mom, can I go talk to Matt?"

There wasn't much else to do. "Sure, honey."

Alayna wasn't handling their arrangement quite as well. "Mom, this is so weird! Couldn't we just find a hotel or something?"

Debbie had wished the same thing more than a few times. "I'm sorry, sweetie, but every hotel is full for three hundred miles. Everyone had to leave their homes." She stroked her daughter's long, brown hair and tried to placate her. "Let's just hope we don't have to stay too long and that the storm doesn't do as much damage as they predict."

Bob caught Debbie's eye. He had tuned his hand-held radio to a local weather station, and his expression was grim. "It doesn't look good so far," he said softly.

Hurricane weather was a new experience for the Coopers. Bob's work had brought them from California to Florida two years earlier. Since then they'd had just one other encounter with a severe hurricane. Fortunately that storm had only done minor roof damage to their house. This time it seemed they wouldn't be so lucky. They could only hope they'd have a home to which they could return.

With nothing to do but sit and wait for the storm to pass, Debbie felt restless. She could see Alayna was reacting similarly, pacing back and forth, her brow furrowed. Debbie could tell she was in deep thought. "What's on your mind, Alayna?"

Her daughter turned to face her. "What if my

music-box collection gets ruined? I'll be so upset. And what about my prom dress?"

Debbie had already lamented over the possibility of losing the new bedroom suite she'd recently purchased, but she was trying to keep a positive attitude for her family. "They're just things," Debbie tried to comfort her daughter. "We'd be sad to lose them, but we can replace them if we have to."

Suddenly Debbie remembered something that couldn't be replaced—that she could hardly bear the thought of losing. *Oh no! The scrapbooks!* If she'd only had more time, she would have brought them to ensure that they'd be protected. A queasy feeling overtook her as she thought of all the time and effort she'd put into preserving their family photos, only to realize they might be destroyed in the hurricane. She decided not to mention it to Alayna. Mother and daughter enjoyed scrapbooking together, and she didn't want to give Alayna cause to fret even more.

Together they sat, silent in remorse over their potential losses. It took several hours before Debbie finally realized she was being self-centered. Hundreds of people in the gym were in the same situation.

Everyone in the room would probably experience some loss from the hurricane, and there were hundreds of shelters just like this one with hundreds, thousands of people in the same predicament. The sheer magnitude of the potential loss changed her perspective a bit. With forced optimism she attempted to look outward instead of focusing on her own situation.

"There are lots of things I hope we still have when we get back home," Debbie said to Alayna and Bob, but mostly to herself. "Just remember, we're not the only ones being evacuated from the storm." She nodded toward their neighbors all around them.

Alayna nodded but sounded defensive. "I know—but I'd take a California earthquake over a Florida hurricane any day!"

■

After four long, anxious nights, the Coopers were given permission to return to their home. The main highway had finally been cleared and was open for travel. As they feared, their neighborhood had been hit hard. Only residents were allowed to enter the

area. Three people who had refused to evacuate had been killed in the storm.

With a mixture of anticipation and dread, the Cooper family drove home. Along the way they stared out the windows, watching the damage to homes worsen the closer they got to their neighborhood.

Two streets from their house, a fallen tree still blocked the road, making it impassable. "OK, let's walk from here," Bob instructed the family. The street was strewn with broken tree branches and rubble. Walking toward their home, Debbie noticed the damage done to neighboring houses. A fallen tree protruded from a huge hole in one roof. Another home looked to be in fairly good condition except for the chimney. Bricks were scattered throughout the yard. She began to feel hopeful that perhaps their home had fared equally well.

"Mom, look at that one!" Aiden exclaimed, pointing to a house that looked like it was cut in half. They could see straight into the three bedrooms along the side of the house.

With more urgency Debbie moved toward their address. If not for the number on the mailbox, she wouldn't have recognized her own home. The hurricane's fierce wind had not only taken their roof, it had swept away the whole second story.

Debbie held a hand to her mouth to muffle the whimper that threatened to escape. Bob opened his arms and pulled his family close. Silently the Coopers comforted each other, their eyes fixed on what little remained of their home.

Suddenly Debbie remembered the scrapbooks. Hurdling debris in the yard, she ran to the house to see if by some miracle they might still be there. Entering their home, she bypassed shattered glass and found more than a foot of water standing throughout what remained of the house. Across the living room, she spotted the bookcase that had held the scrapbooks lying facedown in the water. Slowly, with a sense of total dread, she dragged her feet through the water toward the bookcase. She knew there was no chance that twenty years of their family memories could possibly have endured the storm's devastation. Seeing ruined books scattered everywhere, Debbie could no longer contain her grief for all they had lost.

By then Bob and the kids had caught up with Debbie and found her in tears. Bob put his arm

around her. "What is it?" he demanded, alarmed.

"Oh, Bob, they're gone . . . they're all gone—our memories, our treasures—our past!"

"We've got insurance. We can replace everything," he comforted. But Debbie knew he had no idea what she was talking about.

"Our scrapbooks, Bob," she explained tearfully. "We can't ever replace them."

"Hey, Mom," Alayna interrupted with a shout. "Look over there!" Alayna pointed to a yellow, waterproof duffel bag floating behind the sofa. She sloshed across the room and picked it up. "Mom! It's still here!" she said triumphantly, carrying the dripping bag to her mother.

Debbie recognized the bag from their recent canoe trip but had no idea what was inside. Curious, she unzipped the large bag.

Inside were their scrapbooks, perfectly preserved!

"While you and Dad were rushing around getting ready to evacuate, I remembered that we never finished scrapbooking the pictures from our canoe trip," Alayna explained to her astonished and speechless mother. "I thought it just might help to put those photos and the scrapbooks in the waterproof bag we used on the trip. I knew I wouldn't be able to save my music-box collection, but I thought I might be able to save something important to the whole family."

Debbie stood up and hugged Alayna, feelings of pride in her daughter, gratitude, and joy overwhelming her feelings of grief and loss. Yes, they'd lost a lot. But they still had what was most important—the things that couldn't be replaced. They had each other, and they had their memories. Those things were priceless.

Chapter 7

Giving Love

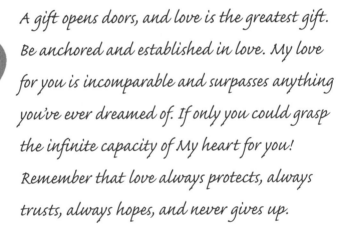

A gift opens doors, and love is the greatest gift.
Be anchored and established in love. My love
for you is incomparable and surpasses anything
you've ever dreamed of. If only you could grasp
the infinite capacity of My heart for you!
Remember that love always protects, always
trusts, always hopes, and never gives up.

With unfailing affection,
Your God of Love

—from Proverbs 18:16; 1 Corinthians 13:13;
Ephesians 3:17–19; 1 Corinthians 13:7

Scrapbooking is a labor of love. The people gracing the pages of your scrapbook are your family and friends. They're the ones who impact your life enough to make you want to photograph them in the first place. The fact that you put them in your book signifies that they are the people for whom you truly care. The countless hours you spend cropping photos and decorating pages shows how much you value those people.

Children especially love to look at pictures of themselves. How often does a mother hear her child's request, "Mom, take my picture!" Their reward (and yours) is holding the photo in hand and marveling at their image. Children may understand even more than adults the clear message of love when someone wants to take their picture. And even more love and value is perceived when someone takes the time and care to showcase those photos in a handcrafted scrapbook.

You communicate love by scrapbooking. Your work demonstrates unquestionably that the people whose activities and accomplishments you chronicle are worth your valuable time and effort. And demonstrating your love for someone is the most important gift of all.

Those gifts are ever the most acceptable
which the giver has made precious.

Ovid

Jessica had held herself

together until that

moment. But suddenly

words gave way to tears of

stress and exhaustion.

The Blessing

Jessica closed her eyes and rested her head on the kitchen counter, waiting for relief from her throbbing headache. She pressed her temples and debated whether to push through her exhaustion and handle the chores she had planned for the day or give up and take a nap.

A rap at the back door ruled out that option. Slowly she raised her head to see her best friend, Lori, wave through the window and let herself in. Lori was always bubbly and energetic, but she toned her mood down immediately when she got a good look at Jessica. She sat on the kitchen stool beside her friend. "Hey, Jessica. How'd it go last night?"

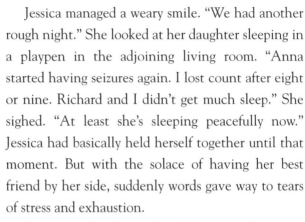

Jessica managed a weary smile. "We had another rough night." She looked at her daughter sleeping in a playpen in the adjoining living room. "Anna started having seizures again. I lost count after eight or nine. Richard and I didn't get much sleep." She sighed. "At least she's sleeping peacefully now." Jessica had basically held herself together until that moment. But with the solace of having her best friend by her side, suddenly words gave way to tears of stress and exhaustion.

Lori immediately enveloped Jessica in her arms, holding on tight. "I'm so sorry, Jessica. You should have called me. I would have been right over to help."

Jessica shook her head. "I'm just so tired of asking for help. It's been ten months of others helping us. I feel indebted to the whole world."

Lori pulled away and looked Jessica straight in the eye, reprimanding the girl she'd known since elementary school. "You should have called me."

Jessica nodded repentantly and smiled slightly but more genuinely this time.

Lori tucked loose strands of hair behind Jessica's ear. "Why don't you get some rest while I do a few things around the house? I'll wake you up if anything happens with Anna. OK?"

Jessica let out a sigh of relief and gratitude. "Thanks, Lori. I don't know what I'd do without you."

Jessica had conceived after many years of infertility. But the initial joy at this news had been quickly overshadowed by fear when tests verified that the baby would be severely retarded and would likely have a host of other disorders.

Although early tests indicated that Anna was not as mentally challenged as they'd expected, she was born with heart defects that required several surgeries to remedy. She was subject to chronic infections and had recently started having seizures. Her little life had started roughly, and it didn't seem to be getting any better. Jessica's initial hopefulness was fading into despair that her baby wouldn't survive to her first birthday—another of the dire predictions.

"Lori, sometimes I just don't think I can handle this. She's so sick! Every day I wonder if it may be the day her little heart decides to quit. Then I wonder why God would let this happen in the first place!"

She couldn't hide the tinge of anger she felt.

Lori was quiet for a minute, then she took Jessica's hand and led her to Anna's playpen. Together they looked over the frail child. Lori knelt and tenderly caressed Anna's forehead. "Jessica, I know it may not feel true right now, but God promises He won't give you more than you can handle." She brushed Anna's cheek with her fingertips and continued softly but confidently. "Look at her, Jessica. She's beautiful!" She looked up at her friend, and Jessica saw the tears that were filling her eyes too.

"God created Anna, and I have no doubt He has a plan for her little life." Lori stood and took Jessica's hands, looking her in the eyes with conviction. "We don't know how long we'll have Anna with us—no one ever knows how long we'll have those we love. So we've got to treat every day as a gift. Last night was tough. Let's pray that today will be better."

■

Later that day Lori stopped by again to check on Jessica and Anna. "How are you doing?"

Jessica smiled and kissed Anna's head as she sat cooing on her lap. "We're both doing much better."

"I'm so glad to hear it." Lori grinned and handed Jessica a completed checklist. "I finished the errands you had . . . and I brought you something." She presented a small scrapbook with a ribbon holding the pages closed.

Jessica couldn't conceal her delight at the surprise. "What's this?"

Anna was already fascinated and batting at the book, and Lori laughed. "Well, it looks like Anna wants to find out, so open it."

Jessica untied the ribbon and opened the scrapbook. The first page featured a picture from Anna's first day of life. Above the photo of the tiny infant was an inscription from the book of Jeremiah: "'I know the plans I have for you,' declares the LORD, 'plans to prosper you and not to harm you, plans to give you hope and a future.'"

Each page showed the milestones of Anna's little life. Her first meeting with her parents. Her first day home after five weeks in the hospital. Her first outing to church services.

"I wanted to wait for Anna's first birthday to give it to you, but I felt you needed it now. I've been collecting photos ever since Anna was born

so I could put together this scrapbook. I knew you wouldn't have time."

Jessica felt hot tears coming again, this time joyful ones. She was overwhelmed by the labor of love her dear friend had displayed. "Thank you, Lori. This is such a special gift! I'll treasure it forever."

Lori reached over and let Anna take a finger in her baby-firm grip. "*This* is a special gift. The scrapbook is so we'll never forget it, no matter what the future holds."

Look for These Other Great Hugs™ Books

Hugs for Mom

Hugs for Kids

Hugs for Sisters

Hugs for Friends

Hugs for Women

Hugs for Grads

Hugs for Grandma

Hugs for Daughters

Hugs for Brothers

Hugs for Girlfriends

Hugs for New Moms

Hugs for Nurses

Hugs for Sons

Hugs for Your Birthday

Hugs for Mom, Book 2

Hugs for Granddaughters

Hugs for Friends, Book 2

Hugs for Dad

Hugs for Teens

Hugs for Teachers

Hugs for Heroes

Hugs for Pet Lovers

Hugs for Women on the Go

Hugs for Coffee Lovers

Hugs for the Hurting

Hugs for Those in Love

Hugs for Grandparents

Hugs for the Holidays

Hugs to Encourage and Inspire

Hugs to Brighten Your Day